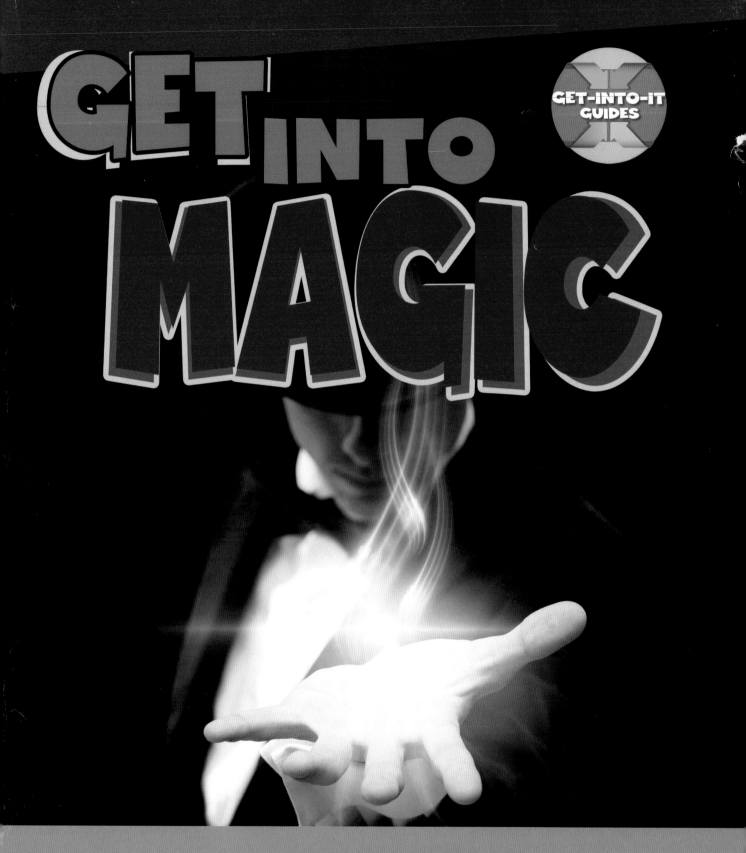

GET INTO MAGIC

GET-INTO-IT GUIDES

VIC KOVACS

CRABTREE
Publishing Company
www.crabtreebooks.com

GET-INTO-IT GUIDES

Author: Vic Kovacs

Editors: Marcia Abramson, Philip Gebhardt

Photo research: Melissa McClellan

Editorial director: Kathy Middleton

Proofreader: Janine Deschenes

Cover/Interior Design: T.J. Choleva

Production coordinator and
   Prepress technician: Samara Parent

Print coordinator: Margaret Amy Salter

Consultant: Drew Dafoe
Director/Producer/Magician, former host and
producer on TVOKids "The Space" (TVOntario), the
daily live after school interactive kids block dedicated
to engaging and educating school-aged children,
including a feature called Drew's Magic Tricks.

Developed and produced for Crabtree Publishing
by BlueApple*Works* Inc.

Photographs

Shutterstock.com: © Fer Gregory (cover top banner); © se media (cover center left);
© Tarzhanova (cover far right); © indigolotos (cover far left top); © Syda Productions (cover
center left bottom); © Real Deal Photo (cover center right); © Nagy-Bagoly Arpad (cover
center right bottom); © kenary820 (cover bottom left); © Tatiana Liubarskaya (cover top right);
© Syda Productions (title page); © Fer Gregory (TOC background); © Be Good (p. 7 top, 14
left, 21 top left, 24 left, 25 top right, 25 bottom left, 28 right); © Ravennka (p. 4, 7, 9, 19, 29
background); © Vava Vladimir Jovanovic (p. 9 top); Axenova Alena (p. 9 bottom); © Botond
Horvath (p. 26 background); © PowerUp (p. 27 bottom left); © Aquir (p. 27 top right);
© JSvector (p. 27 bottom);

Public Domain: p. 5 top, 5 bottom, 6 top, Library of Congress (p. 6 bottom), p. 7 bottom, Jasper
Maskelyne (p. 19 bottom); Strobridge Litho. Co., Library of Congress (p. 25 left); Pfc. Joshua
Grant/United States Marine Corps. (p. 29 top);

Creative Commons: Bryan Derballa (p. 7 middle); Janellesutton (p. 8);
Angela George (p. 28 left);

© Austen Photography (TOC, p. 4, 10, 11,12, 13, 14, 15, 16, 17, 18, 19, 20, 21, 22, 23, 24, 25, 29
left, 31, back cover)

Library and Archives Canada Cataloguing in Publication

Kovacs, Vic, author
        Get into magic / Vic Kovacs.

(Get-into-it guides)
Includes index.
Issued in print and electronic formats.
ISBN 978-0-7787-3401-7 (hardcover).—
ISBN 978-0-7787-3405-5 (softcover).--
ISBN 978-1-4271-1914-8 (HTML)

        1. Magic tricks--Juvenile literature. 2. Tricks--Juvenile
literature.
I. Title.

GV1548.K68 2017   j793.8   C2016-907384-X
                                         C2016-907385-8

Library of Congress Cataloging-in-Publication Data

CIP available at the Library of Congress.

Crabtree Publishing Company

www.crabtreebooks.com   1-800-387-7650

Printed in Canada/032017/BF20170111

Published in Canada
Crabtree Publishing
616 Welland Ave.
St. Catharines, Ontario
L2M 5V6

Published in the United States
Crabtree Publishing
PMB 59051
350 Fifth Avenue, 59th Floor
New York, New York 10118

Published in the United Kingdom
Crabtree Publishing
Maritime House
Basin Road North, Hove
BN41 1WR

Published in Australia
Crabtree Publishing
3 Charles Street
Coburg North
VIC, 3058

CONTENTS

MAGIC THROUGH TIME

For thousands of years, human beings have tried to use **rituals** and **symbols** to influence events and change situations for their benefit. These practices eventually came to be known as magic.

People also practiced another form of magic, called conjuring. Known today as stage, street, or practical magic, this kind of magic uses clever tricks to create the **illusion** of impossible **feats**.

EARLY DAYS OF MAGIC

The earliest known magic trick was performed in Ancient Egypt almost five thousand years ago. That illusion is known today as the cups and balls trick. It was still being performed in Rome about three thousand years later. During the **Middle Ages**, the first books showing how to perform various illusions were published. At the same time, magic was often used by gamblers to gain an advantage. Other people used it as a way to convince people that they possessed great and mysterious powers. The Middle Ages was a time when some people, such as circus performers, began using illusions to entertain audiences.

How To Use This Book

The magic tricks in this book are meant to inspire you to get into magic, to keep learning, and to create your own magic tricks. You can follow the steps provided, or use your imagination to modify the tricks using different **props** and ideas.

Abracadabra *is a magic word often used in stage magic tricks. Many years ago, people believed the word had healing powers!*

Occult And Witchcraft

The study of **paranormal** abilities and practices, or things that cannot be explained by science, is known as **occultism**. **Witchcraft** is the practice of performing spells and rituals. Because early illusionists seemed to perform impossible feats, such as causing objects to vanish, many of them were associated

During the Middle Ages, witchcraft was illegal in many countries. The punishment was death. Thousands of people accused of witchcraft were executed, many of them by being burned at the stake.

with both witchcraft and occultism. Performers also often claimed to possess magical powers, which helped to confirm these beliefs.

In 1584, an Englishman named Reginald Scot published a book titled *The Discoverie Of Witchcraft*. It included a section that showed that many feats of witchcraft were simply tricks performed by people attempting to fool the audience. His book was one of the earliest publications that explained how magic was performed. However, witchcraft and magic remained **controversial**, and many copies of his book were burned.

Chung Ling Soo

Much of magic is based on **deception** and illusion, but some magicians go even further than you might imagine when tricking their audience. Take the story of Chung Ling Soo. Chung Ling Soo was a popular magician in the early 1900s. He claimed to be half Chinese, and to have been raised by a Chinese magician. In reality, he was a white American named William E. Robinson who had copied much of his act from the actual Chinese magician named Ching Ling Foo. However, his deception was so convincing that most of the public didn't find out his true identity until after his death.

Chung Ling Soo died in 1918 while performing a faulty bullet catch trick.

STAGE MAGIC

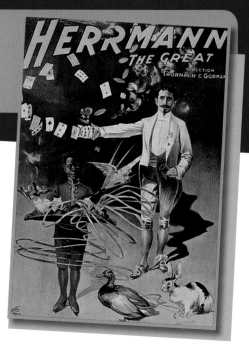

Modern stage magic didn't begin to take shape until the 1800s. Before then, it was usually performed at fairs by traveling magicians. In 1845, the French magician Jean Eugene Robert-Houdin opened a magic theater in Paris. Others followed in London, Glasgow, and elsewhere. Having theaters designed for magic allowed magicians to perform previously unthinkable illusions.

Alexander Herrmann was one of the most popular magicians of the late 19th century. Better known as Herrmann the Great, he was famous for his spectacular shows throughout North America and Europe.

20TH CENTURY MAGIC

The first half of the 20th century was considered a golden age for stage magic. Many magicians worked their way up through the ranks, starting off as **apprentices** to other magicians while learning the craft. From there they would develop (or steal) illusions and create their own shows. Howard Thurston, one of the greatest magicians of all time, developed a show so massive it took eight train cars just to transport it. Eventually, with the rise of movies, the popularity of magic declined. Some magicians were able to move to television, and created early versions of **special effects** to produce new illusions. But magic performances were no longer the grand spectacles they had once been.

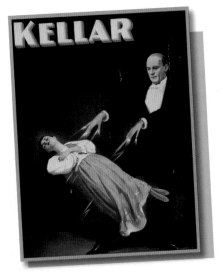

*Harry Kellar was an American magician who performed during the late 19th and early 20th centuries. One of his best known illusions was the **levitation** of a female assistant.*

New Era of Magic

Magic became popular again in the 1970s. Beginning with Canadian magician Doug Henning's popular Broadway show in 1974, big stage magic entered a new era. Much of this new golden age centered on Las Vegas, where huge stage shows remain popular today. Performers such as Siegfried and Roy, David Copperfield, and Penn and Teller all produced giant, astounding new shows.

Today, magic has undergone another revitalization, with illusionists such as David Blaine, Criss Angel, and others using a style of performance known as street magic. They record

performances in which they perform tricks for unsuspecting bystanders on the street, who are often shocked and amazed.

*David Blaine is an American magician best known for his high-profile feats of **endurance**. In 2012, he performed a 72-hour endurance stunt during which he was "electrified" by one million volts of electricity.*

Father Of Modern Magic

Jean Eugene Robert-Houdin is often called the father of modern magic. Born in France in 1805, he originally trained as a watchmaker. He was one of the first magicians to wear **evening wear** such as tuxedos. Possibly his most important contribution was his 1845 opening of a magic theater. He took magic off the street and combined it with the dignity of the theater. The theater also made it possible to build more complex illusions that could only be done on a stage that was designed specifically for the trick.

Houdin's influence was so great that famous magician Harry Houdini, pictured right, based his performing name on Houdin.

PRINCIPLES OF MAGICAL EFFECTS

Misdirection is when a magician directs the audience's attention to one point in order to distract them from looking where the actual trick is being performed. Misdirection is one of the most important concepts in almost all illusions, and can be achieved a number of ways. Magicians might make a big, showy gesture with their left hand to distract the audience from what the right hand is doing. Or they might convince the audience that something is important, while the trick is being performed elsewhere. A good magician can use misdirection to direct their audience's attention to flow from one point to another like water, never seeing anything they're not meant to see.

Many magicians also use assistants who not only help them set up their tricks, but can also be essential for misdirection and sometimes are even the focus of the tricks themselves!

KEY PRINCIPLES USED IN MAGICAL EFFECTS

In addition to misdirection, there are other key principles used in magical effects. Most basic tricks can be classified based on what effect they appear to achieve.

SLEIGHT OF HAND

Sleight of hand is a key skill that magicians have to master. It involves hand movements that hide the magician's intentions. Sleight of hand is used in most magical tricks and effects.

TELEPORTATION

These tricks seem to cause a person or object to move from one point to another. For example, a coin might disappear from one hand, only to appear in the other.

PRODUCTION

This effect seems to create something where previously there was nothing. Pulling a coin from thin air is a production effect.

VANISHING

This is the opposite of production. In this kind of illusion, a seemingly solid object is made to disappear. David Copperfield's famous trick in which he caused the Statue of Liberty to disappear was a particularly huge vanishing trick.

RESTORATION

These tricks appear to magically fix something that has been broken. A magician might cut a handkerchief in half, only to make it whole again a moment later.

PREDICTION

Sometimes called mind-reading, these illusions make it appear that the magician has knowledge that they seemingly couldn't have.

TRANSFORMATION

These tricks seem to change one thing into something else. A popular example is turning a stuffed rabbit into a real one.

LEVITATION

These illusions make it appear that a person or object is floating above the ground without any assistance.

ESCAPOLOGY

This is the art of getting out of seemingly impossible restraints. This might be as simple as escaping from a pair of handcuffs, or as complicated as getting out of a straitjacket while locked in a tank full of water.

Basic tricks usually use only one type of effect, while more complex ones might include several effects. Some magicians combine different effects to create a spellbinding illusion, while many other magicians choose one as their special focus. For example, Harry Houdini was a gifted magician, but he became famous for his skills as an escapologist who was able to get out of anything. Whatever the type of trick you're performing, it will require a degree of setup, and a whole lot of practice. Some even need an assistant to help out!

OUTFITS AND PROPS

When most people think of a magician, the image that usually pops into their head is a person in formal wear, such as a tuxedo, often holding a top hat and a magic wand. There's a reason this became such a universal image of magic. Many magicians prefer wearing suits because their long sleeves, multiple pockets, and other features provide many places to hide the props for their act. When making something disappear, they just have to drop the object into their pocket without letting the audience see it.

The magic wand also has a very practical use in stage magic: misdirection. While the audience concentrates on the wand, they're not looking at what the magician's free hand is doing.

Other famous magical props include the cups and balls, playing cards, and dice.

SLEIGHT OF HAND

Tip

Practice your magic tricks in front of a mirror. It will give you a better idea of what your audience can see. Change or adjust your techniques if you notice moves that are not supposed to be seen.

Sleight of hand can refer to a number of different techniques. It involves small, quick, hand-and-finger movements that distract the audience and mask the magician's aims. Many tricks rely on sleight of hand. Beginning magicians should spend hours practicing and perfecting sleight of hand techniques. One of the easiest and most commonly used sleight of hand techniques is called the French Drop.

Effect

With this technique, you'll be able to make it appear as if a coin has vanished into thin air!

THE FRENCH DROP

You Will Need:
- 1 large coin

SOME OT THE PRINCIPLES OF SLEIGHT OF HAND

Ditch - Making an object disappear without anyone noticing.

Load - Moving an object wherever you want it to be.

Misdirection - Leading your audience's attention away from your moves.

Palm - Holding an object in your hand without anyone noticing.

Simulation - Creating an illusion of activity that hasn't happened.

Switch - Secretly switching one object for another.

1 For this trick, all you'll need is a coin. Larger coins, such as a half or silver dollar, work well, but you can also use a quarter.

2 In your **dominant hand**, grasp the coin between your first finger and your thumb. Your thumb should be on top, with your palm facing up. The face of the coin should be facing outward, toward your audience.

3 With your other hand, reach toward the coin, with that hand's thumb coming behind the coin and its fingers passing in front.

CARD TRICKS USING SLEIGHTS

Magicians use sleights for card tricks so that the audience does not notice what is really happening. Card tricks take lots of practice to perfect.

THE SHIFT

Effect
The volunteer places a card in the middle of the deck. The magician moves the card to the top of the deck without the volunteer noticing.

1 Have a volunteer choose a card. Hold half the deck of cards in your left hand, and have the volunteer put the card on top.

2 Use your left pinky to mark the card. Then place the other half of the deck on top with your right hand.

3 With one smooth motion, grab the bottom part of the deck with your right hand and the top part with your left hand and reverse positions. Use your hands and the new top part of the deck to hide the switch.

You Will Need:

■ 1 deck of cards

4 As your non-dominant hand goes to close over the coin, raise the thumb holding the coin and allow the coin to drop into the fingers of your dominant hand.

5 Close your non-dominant hand as if it has grasped the coin, and move it away. Keep your dominant hand open, but angled in such a way that the audience cannot see the coin inside of it.

6 For the reveal, open your non-dominant hand, showing that the coin has seemingly disappeared.

TELEPORTATION MAGIC

Teleportation tricks make it appear as if a person or object has magically moved from one location to another. A teleportation illusion might be as simple as causing a coin to move from one hand to another without the hands touching, or as spectacular as causing an assistant to disappear from a stage, only to suddenly appear at the back of the theater. Many teleportation tricks are made up of two parts: the vanish and the production. The Jumping Rubber Band trick is a great place to start.

JUMPING RUBBER BAND

You Will Need: ■ *1 rubber band*

Effect
Teleport a rubber band from the first two fingers on your hand to the last two!

For this trick, all you need is a rubber band. Place the rubber band around the base of your first and middle fingers on either hand.

Showing the audience the back of your hand, stretch out the rubber band away from your palm, to show that it's really on those fingers.

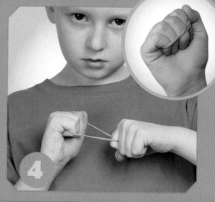

While stretching the rubber band, close the hand it's on into a fist.

While doing this, slip the backs of your ring and pinky fingers into the rubber band. But, do not show steps 3 and 4 to the audience. Turn your hand towards you to do that.

MOVING COINS TRICK

This simple teleportation trick is based on speed. Move the coin quicker than your audience's eyes can see!

Effect

Teleport a coin from one hand to another!

SHIFTING COIN

You Will Need:
- 1 coin
- 1 soft surface

Hold your hands palms up on a soft surface. Place a coin in your dominant hand close to your index finger and thumb, as shown.

Turn your hands over as fast as you can to make the coin fly from one hand to another. Practice this move until you're really quick with the move.

If done right, the coin should be under your other hand. The soft surface is used to muffle any sounds the flipping coin might make.

Turn your dominant hand over and show the audience that the coin has vanished.

Turn your other hand over and show the audience that the coin has teleported over.

To the audience, it should appear that the rubber band is just around the base of your first two fingers, but the side facing you will have all four fingers in the band.

To complete the trick, straighten your fingers back up. The band will jump to your middle and pinky fingers instantly!

Tip

You can cause the rubber band to jump back to your middle and first fingers by repeating these steps.

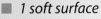

13

VANISHING MAGIC

Vanishing tricks are exactly what they sound like: a magician causes an object to disappear. In close-up magic, this is usually achieved with a clever combination of sleight of hand and misdirection. Larger illusions, such as causing a person to vanish, might involve mirrors, giant cabinets, and trap doors! Since you probably don't have access to any of those yet, we're going to use some standard household objects you probably already have.

VANISHING SALTSHAKER

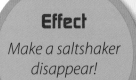

Effect
Make a saltshaker disappear!

You Will Need:
- paper towel or tissue paper
- 1 coin
- 1 saltshaker or plastic cup

ABRACADABRA

This trick also incorporates "patter," which is when a magician talks the audience through what they're doing. Patter is an important part of all magic tricks. Using the right words can help make your simple magic trick into a real theatrical event.

1 To start, place your saltshaker or cup on top of your coin, on a table top. Tell the audience that you're going to make the coin disappear.

2 Then, place the paper towel over the saltshaker or cup so that it's totally covered and grip it around the middle, so the shape of the saltshaker can be seen.

3 Say some magic words and bring the covered saltshaker toward you. The coin is still on the table.

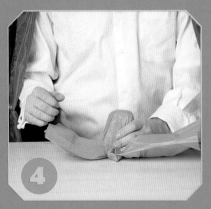

4 Place the covered saltshaker back on top of the coin.

5

Tell the audience that sometimes it's hard to make the coin disappear. Tell them that instead, you're going to make the saltshaker disappear.

6

While telling them this, bring the covered saltshaker back toward you. Keep the bottom of it just under the table, and relax your grip slightly. The saltshaker will slip into your lap, but the paper towel will keep its shape.

7

Show the audience the now empty paper towel. Voilà! The saltshaker has "vanished!"

VANISHING COIN

This vanishing trick takes advantage of optical misdirection. The audience will not be able to see the paper circle glued to the cup because it will blend with the bottom sheet.

You Will Need:
- 1 clear plastic cup
- 2 sheets of paper
- pencil
- scissors
- glue
- piece of cloth
- 1 coin

1

Place a clear plastic cup on a sheet of paper as shown. Trace around the rim, then cut the paper circle out.

2

Glue the paper circle to the rim of the cup. If there are any uneven edges, trim them off with scissors.

Effect

Make a coin disappear!

3

Prepare your set as shown. Ask a member of the audience for a coin to make your performance more impressive.

4

Place the cloth over the cup to cover it fully. Lift the cloth and the cup together and place it over the coin.

5

Loosen your grip on the cloth and lift it, leaving the cup behind. The coin will be hidden under the paper circle, but to the audience it will look as if it vanished.

6

Tell your volunteer not to worry about the missing coin. Say, "Abracadabra," put the cloth back over the cup, lift it, and the coin will reappear.

PRODUCTION MAGIC

Production tricks are the exact opposite of vanishing illusions. Instead of causing something to disappear, production tricks make it look as if something has appeared! An example is pulling a coin or handkerchief out of thin air or out of other objects. A hat is often used as a prop to pull objects out of. Pulling a rabbit out of a hat is a typical example. A skilled magician can even "produce" himself or herself, appearing in a puff of smoke on a stage. Often, an audience member will be invited onstage to examine the magician's props and make sure he or she isn't hiding anything up their sleeves.

MAGIC MAGAZINE

You Will Need:

- magazine or newspaper
- 1 matchbox sleeve
- piece of cardstock
- 1 silk handkerchief
- piece of string
- glue or tape
- scissors

Effect
Make a handkerchief fly out of a magazine!

1 Tie a piece of string about about 10 inches (25 cm) long to one corner of a silk handkerchief.

2 Cut a piece of carrdstock about 1 inch (2.5 cm) wide by 4 inches (10 cm) long. Tape or glue it to the matchbox as shown.

PROPS

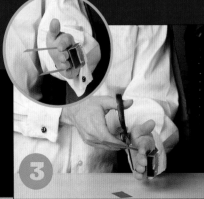

3 Hold the cardstock strip between your fingers as shown and trim the protruding ends. Make sure that the ends of the strip don't show, but you still can hold the strip between your fingers securely.

4 Tuck all of the handkerchief with the string into the matchbox sleeve. Leave a short piece of string hanging out.

5 Practice holding the prop in front of a mirror as shown. Make sure your audience will not be able to see the box or the strip between your fingers.

ENGAGING YOUR AUDIENCE

The way you say your words will have an effect on your audience. Make sure to practice speaking clearly and loudly, and never use a **monotone**. You might want to record yourself as you talk during a practice performance. When you listen to yourself afterwards, ask yourself: Do you like what you hear? Is your voice loud enough? Are you speaking clearly? Do you sound confident?

Tip
Try finding a magazine or a catalog showing a string on a page. Tell your audience "Wait a minute, it looks like there is a piece of string coming out of this page?!" Then do your trick and make them gasp in amazement!

Pick up your magazine. Stand with the side of your body facing the audience and keep your left hand with the prop box hidden from view as shown.

Pretend that you're looking at something on the page and tear a little hole in the magazine close to your hidden hand with your visible hand. (Optional: Tear a hole in the magazine before your performance.)

With a surprised look, reach through the hole with your fingers and grab the end of the string. Slowly and carefully, begin to pull the string out with a look of disbelief.

9 *Keep pulling the string out until you reach the tip of the handkerchief.*

10 *Look bewildered and say something like "Wait, it's not just the string, there is more stuff coming out of this magzine!"*

11 *Grab the tip of the handkerchief and give it a sudden sharp tug. Finish your trick with a theatrical handwave and a bow.*

RESTORATION MAGIC

Restoration magic involves two parts. In the first part, the magician presents the audience with a normal object, which is then torn, broken, or otherwise destroyed. In the second part, the magician fixes the object, restoring it to its original form. This next trick is a type of restoration illusion called a cut and restore. It requires a bit of preparation, but it is sure to impress your audience.

Keep It Safe

Always check with an adult before using sharp objects!

STRING IN A STRAW

You Will Need:

- straw
- piece of string
- scissors

Effect

Magically reconnect two halves of a cut string!

Before performing the trick, cut a 2-inch (5-cm) slit in the middle of the straw.

To perform the trick, thread the string through the straw. Do not let your audience see the slit.

Once the straw is in the middle of the string, hold it up to the audience. Pull the string tight from both ends to show that it's really in the straw.

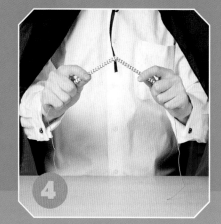

With one smooth motion, bend the straw in half with both hands, angling the slit towards you. Hold it with one hand and while bringing the other hand away, give one end of the sting a quick tug.

The middle of the string should now be outside the slit, but angled in such a way that the audience cannot see it.

6 Pick up your scissors with your free hand, and cut the middle of the straw, above the string.

7 As soon as you make the cut, cover the cut straw with your left hand.

8 After placing the scissors down, wave your right hand over your fist and say some magic words.

9 Then, while still holding the middle of the straw, pull out the string. It appears as if the two halves of the string have been magically put back together.

MASTER OF RESTORATION

P.T. Selbit is remembered today as the creator of one of the most iconic magic tricks of all time: sawing a woman in half. However, the trick itself is actually fairly simple! After asking his assistant to get into a wooden box and lie down, the magician saws the box, and his assistant, in half.

After separating the two halves, the assistant's legs are shown as still able to move! The boxes are then placed together, magic words are said, and the assistant exits without even a scar. How? Well, the box is actually two boxes. In the lower box, a second hidden assistant is curled up. When the main assistant gets into the top box, the hidden assistant puts their legs through the holes in the second box, and removes them at the end when the main assistant gets out of the box!

P.T. Selbit performing the sawing a woman in half illusion.

PREDICTION MAGIC

We all know that it is impossible to see into the future or to read someone's mind. Prediction magic uses a few clever tricks to make it seem real. Prediction techniques, like many mechanisms behind magic, are often very simple. Prediction tricks also almost always involve audience participation, which is a fun way to make a show more personal.

Effect

Predict the color of a crayon picked by a volunteer.

You Will Need:
- *crayons*
- *pouch or bag*
- *volunteer*

GUESS THE COLOR OF A CRAYON

1

Place different-colored crayons in a bag. Ask your volunteer to pick one.

2

Turn around and ask the volunteer to place the crayon in your hand.

3

Turn around to face the volunteer again. Scrape the crayon with your thumbnail gently, just enough to get some of the color to leave a mark on your nail. Turn around again and ask the volunteer to take the crayon back.

4 *Ask the volunteer to place the crayon back into the pouch. Do not look at the crayon.*

5 *Hold the pouch in front of you with your thumb facing you as shown. Pretend that you are trying hard to see through the pouch.*

6 *While doing that, check the color smear on your thumbnail, then tell the volunteer which crayon he or she picked.*

MENTAL MAGIC

Prediction magic tricks can use a word, a number, or an event—or a combination of these things. Sometimes the prediction involves something that only the audience should know. The following prediction trick is based on mathematics. It makes it look as if you can predict numbers. Rest assured, your friends and audience will be astounded every time!

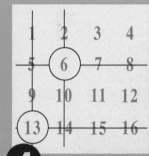

Effect

Regardless of what numbers your audience will pick, the final total will always be number 34!

ABRACADABRA

Have fun and be confident when talking to the audience. Learn how to use humor in your performances; it guarantees a happy audience. Work jokes into your routine and patter.

MAGIC NUMBER - 34

You Will Need:

- sheet of paper with your number grid
- thick paper marked with number 34
- marker ■ 1 volunteer from the audience

1 *Before you begin, write the number 34 on a piece of thick paper. Fold it and tell your volunteer that you know what number will be the final outome of the number selections.*

2 *Draw a grid of numbers from 1 to 16 on a sheet of paper as shown.*

3 *Ask your volunteer to pick any number from the grid. Circle the number and cross out the column and the row the number is a part of as shown.*

4 *Ask the volunteer to pick another number from the ones that have not been crossed through. Circle the number and cross out the column and the row.*

7 *Unfold your prediction number sheet and watch your volunteer gasp in surprise. The total of numbers will equal your predicted number 34!*

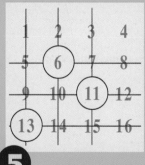

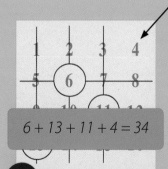

$6 + 13 + 11 + 4 = 34$

5 *Ask for one more number from the ones that have not been crossed out. Circle the number and cross out the lines as was done in steps 3 and 4.*

6 *In our case, the only remaining uncrossed number is 4. Ask your volunteer to add this number to all circled numbers that were picked previously.*

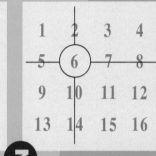

34

TRANSFORMATION MAGIC

Transformation illusions can use a variety of props, from cards and coins to live animals! Whatever the props, the effect is the same: to make it appear that one object is turning into another right in front of your audience's eyes. While turning a rabbit into a dove might be a little advanced, the next trick will show you how to turn one small coin into two larger ones with nothing more than some clever sleight of hand.

Effect

Turn one small coin into two large ones!

DOUBLING COINS

You Will Need:

- 1 smaller coin, such as a nickel
- 2 larger coins of the same type, such as quarters.

1

Hold the two larger coins together, in between your index finger and thumb horizontally.

2

Place the smaller coin in front of the larger ones, vertically. When you hold the smaller coin out for your audience to see, it should block the larger coins from view.

3

Show the audience that your free hand is empty. Then, quickly bring the free hand in front of the coins, sliding the smaller coin along with it and pushing it behind the larger coins with your thumb.

4

Allow the smaller coin to fall into the palm of the hand holding the coins. Take one of the larger coins with the thumb and index finger of your empty hand.

5

In the same quick motion, slide the other larger coin between the thumb and index finger of the hand that was holding the coins. Where once there was a nickel, you suddenly have two quarters!

MAGIC ICE

You Will Need:
- 1 paper cup
- piece of sponge
- scissors
- glass of water
- few ice cubes

Effect

Turn water in a cup into ice instantly!

Cut a round piece of sponge and place it on the bottom of the paper cup. Make sure it fits snugly. Trim the edges if necessary.

Place a few ice cubes on the sponge. Make sure that they don't melt before you perform your trick. Melted ice would add too much water to the sponge.

Pour a little water into your magic cup in front of your audience. The water will be absorbed by the sponge in the cup.

4 Say Abracadabra or some other magic words and turn the cup upside down. Ice will pour out instead of water! Then scrunch the cup and throw it away for a better effect.

Tip

Before you start your trick, experiment with your sponge to find out how much water it can absorb to make the effect just perfect.

LEVITATION AND ESCAPOLOGY MAGIC

Levitation and escapology have one thing in common: they usually use specialized props and materials that a beginning magician isn't likely to have. Levitation, which creates the illusion that an object or person is floating in midair, often uses wires, special harnesses, motorized lifts, and even cranes. Just like other magic effects, this illusion depends on the magician's misdirection, optical illusions, and acting to take the audience's attention away from what is really happening. There are many ways magicians can create the illusion of levitation, but most of them rely on cleverly disguised props and machines.

Escapology involves getting out of restraints such as handcuffs or a straitjacket. Sometimes it includes being locked inside a space such as a tank filled with water. As a result, escapology can be one of the most dangerous branches of magic. The most famous magician of all time, Houdini, was an incredibly talented escapologist. However, like much of magic, many escape tricks involve a very simple concept: either a hidden key, or a skill at lock picking. Houdini was famous for showing up in towns and having the local police lock him in the town jail. Without fail, he was able to escape, to the delight of the townsfolk.

CARD TRICKS

Card tricks are one of the most well-known magical disciplines. Any magician knows at least a few good card tricks, and some even spend their entire careers perfecting and creating new ones. Card tricks can be as simple or as complicated as the magician is comfortable with. Many card tricks involve a combination of different magical techniques. The following trick is many magicians' first card illusion, and involves both sleight of hand and elements of prediction.

PICK THE RIGHT CARD

You Will Need:

■ a deck of cards

Effect
Find the hidden card that a volunteer picked in a deck of cards!

1 Cut the deck of cards a few times, moving half the deck from the top to the bottom.

2 The last time you cut the deck, make sure you get a look at the card that's going on the bottom without your audience seeing that you're doing so.

3 That bottom card is going to be your "marker" card. Remember what it is.

4 Ask for a volunteer and fan out the cards toward them. Ask them to choose a card and remove it from the deck. Tell them to look at it and memorize it, but not to show it to you or tell you what it is.

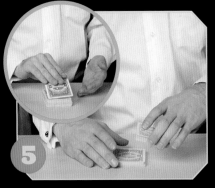

5 Next, place their card on the top of the deck. Cut the deck once. Now, their card will be just underneath your marker card in the middle of the deck.

Cut the deck once more, but make sure you do it above where your marker card is so you don't move its place.

Now, tell your volunteer you are going to find their card and start flipping cards over from the top of the deck.

Once you see your marker card, you know the next card is the one your volunteer picked.

Ask your volunteer "How much do you want to bet the next card I flip is yours?" and reveal their card from the top of the deck.

Tip

You can also do a variation where you continue flipping a few cards after theirs has been revealed. After flipping a few extras, ask them the same question about the next card you flip being theirs. Then reach into the pile and flip theirs face down.

THE KING OF CARDS

During the first few decades of the 20th century, Howard Thurston was probably the most famous magician in the world. He was a **contemporary**, and rival, of Harry Houdini, and was actually better known than the escapologist at the time. While he would eventually put together one of the largest touring stage shows of all time, he first rose to prominence with his innovative card tricks. His signature card trick was the Rising Card, in which he was able to make several cards chosen by audience members float into the air after shuffling them back into the deck. For this and other remarkable illusions, he was known as the King of Cards!

MATH TRICKS

Math tricks are a popular branch of magic that involve numbers. Most could also be considered prediction illusions. They rely on clever tricks and continuous patterns to keep your audience from thinking about them too much. Many people, young and old, find math tricks interesting. They are fun to perform, and help with learning and practicing math skills.

GUESSING AGE AND SHOE SIZES

❶ Ask for a volunteer from the audience. Give them a piece of paper and tell them to write down their age, but not tell it to you.

❷ Tell them to multiply their age by 5. Let them use a calculator if they want to.

❸ Once they have the new number, tell them to write a zero at the end of the answer. The secret here is that this is the same as multiplying by 10, but phrasing it differently makes it more difficult for the volunteers to follow the trick.

❹ Once they have it, tell them to add today's date. Tell them to use only the day's number and to ignore the month and the year. For example if today's date is April 16, 2017, ask them to add only 16.

❺ Tell them to double the number.

❻ Then ask the volunteer to write down their shoe size and to add it to their last number. (Ask them to round up their shoe size number if it's not a whole number.)

❼ Multiply today's date number (remember, it was 16 in our example) by 2 in your head and ask the volunteer to subtract the number you came up with from their last number.

❽ Prepare your volunteer for the finale. Ask them to read the final number out loud. The first part of the number shows their age, and the last two digits are their shoe size.

EXAMPLE

❶ Say, their age is 13.

❷ $13 \times 5 = 65$

❸ Adding a zero to 65 makes 650.

❹ Say, if today is April 16th, the volunteer adds $650 + 16 = 666$.

❺ $666 \times 2 = 1332$

❻ Say, the volunteer's shoe size is 6, they'll add $1332 + 6 = 1338$.

❼ Say, it's April 16th in our example, so multiply $16 \times 2 = 32$ in your head. Tell the volunteer to subtract 32 from their total. $1338 - 32 = 1306$.

❽ 1306;
13 is the age and
06 (6) is the shoe size.

Effect
Reveal the age and shoe size of your volunteer correctly every time!

Effect

Predict what country and what animal your volunteer is thinking of.

❶ Ask for a volunteer from the audience. Tell them to pick a secret number in their minds, but not tell it to you. Tell them to double the number, then add 8 to it. Then have them divide the number in half. Finally, have them subtract their original, secret number from this one.

❷ Now, tell your volunteer to think of the letter of the alphabet that corresponds to their final number. For example, 1 would be A, 2 would be B, and so on.

❸ Once they have the letter, have them think of a country that starts with that letter. Then, have them take the second letter of the name of that country. Once they have it, ask them to envision an animal that lives in that country, and picture the color of that animal.

❹ Once they have it, tell them that you know what they're thinking, but it doesn't make any sense. After all, there are no gray elephants in Denmark.

❺ The key to this trick is moving your volunteer through the sequence fairly quickly. Occasionally you'll get someone who chooses another "D" country, such as the Dominican Republic, or another animal. However, 99% of people choose Denmark and Elephant

INCREDIBLE DICE CALCULATIONS

❶ For this trick, you'll need at least two six-sided dice and a volunteer. Ask your volunteer to pick two dice and roll them one by one. Before they roll, turn around so that you can't see the result of their rolls. Once they have rolled them, tell them to stack one die on top of the other.

❷ Once they tell you they've stacked them, turn back around and look at the number on top of the top die. Explain to your audience that there are three hidden sides of the dice: the side touching the table, and the two sides touching each other. You're going to predict what those sides add up to.

Effect

Roll the dice. Then predict what the hidden sides of the dice add up to!

❸ Here's the secret: opposite sides on a die always add up to 7. So, 1 will always be opposite 6, 2 will always be opposite 5, and 3 will always be opposite 4.

❹ Knowing this, you're going to know that the hidden faces of the bottom dice will always add up to 7. To find out the value of the remaining hidden side, just subtract the number facing up on the top die from 7. Then, add that to 7 and write it down on a piece of paper, and fold it up.

❺ Next, ask your volunteer to add up the hidden faces. Once they do, have them open your prediction and read it to the audience. They'll be shocked that the two numbers match!

Hidden total
8

Hidden total
13

Hidden total
9

BEHIND THE SCENES

It takes many skills to become a master magician, but the most important is dedication. A magician must spend countless hours practicing and perfecting their act. Before ever stepping in front of an audience, a magician must do the same trick again and again until it is **second nature**. Even after perfecting a trick, it needs to be constantly rehearsed so it stays fresh in the magician's mind. Some beginners learn from more experienced magicians. Whatever path you choose, the magician's life is one of constant study and practice.

ABRACADABRA

You will amaze and entertain your audience with even simple tricks if you perform them well. Make sure you are comfortable with a few simple tricks before trying more elaborate and complex ones.

Penn & Teller are American magicians and entertainers. At their popular performances they combine elements of comedy with magic.

MASTERING THE STAGE

Beyond technical skills such as sleight of hand and misdirection, a magician also must become a master of **stagecraft**. A magician is a performer, and must be comfortable and confident in front of a crowd. Developing a **stage persona**, writing engaging patter, and having the confidence to convince your audience of your abilities are all essential skills. Some magicians, such as Teller, of Penn and Teller, are so confident and **charismatic** that they're able to captivate their audience without ever saying a single word.

WHERE TO LEARN MAGIC

There are a number of organizations that are dedicated to the art of magic. These groups promote the performance and study of magic, and connect magicians with each other and with audiences. Some, like the Society of American Magicians, even have youth organizations that can help young magicians learn and grow as practitioners. If you're interested in getting more into magic, it's a good idea to see if there is a magic organization in your area.

Magic conventions are great places to discover magic or learn new ideas, as well as to exchange material, tricks, and ideas.

CODE OF SILENCE

Ever since magic became an accepted performing art, there has been a version of the Magician's **Oath**. While there are different variations, the core of the oath is a promise not to reveal how tricks are done to any non-magicians. This code of silence is taken very seriously by magicians all over the world. After all, if everyone knew how tricks were done, there would be no interest in seeing them performed. So, before you ever perform for an audience, repeat these words:

"As a magician I promise never to reveal the secret to any illusion to a non-magician, unless that one swears to uphold the oath in turn. I promise to never perform any illusion for any non-magician without first practicing the effect until I can perform it well enough to maintain the illusion of magic."

LEARNING MORE

Books

Big Magic for Little Hands: 25 Astounding Illusions for Young Magicians by Joshua Jay, Workman Publishing Company, 2014.

Children's Book Of Magic by DK Publishing, DK Children, 2014.

Kids' Magic Secrets: Simple Magic Tricks And Why They Work by Loris Bree, Marlor Press, 2003.

Magic Up Your Sleeve: Amazing Illusions, Tricks, and Science Facts You'll Never Believe by Helaine Becker, Owlkids Books, 2010.

Mathemagic! Number Tricks by Lynda Colgan, Kids Can Press, 2011.

Websites

Kidzone
www.kidzone.ws/magic/

Visit this site to learn easy magic tricks.

Magic Tricks for Kids
http://magictricksforkids.org/

Magic Tricks for Kids is a friendly, online information hub for children aged 6 to 14 who are either students of magic or are looking to learn how to do magic tricks.

Funology
www.funology.com/magic-tricks/

Some interesting magic tricks to learn are available at this site.

GLOSSARY

aka Short version of "also known as"

apprentice Someone who is learning skills from an expert

charismatic Having special charm or appeal

contemporary A person of the same time period

controversial Causing much discussion especially by opposing views

deception Tricking someone into believing something is true when it is false

dominant hand The hand a person usually uses to write with

endurance The ability to do something difficult for a long time

evening wear Formal clothes such as tuxedos or gowns worn on special occasions

feat An act that shows courage, strength, or skill

illusion Something that deceives or misleads people

levitation The act of lifting a person by means that seem supernatural

Middle Ages The period in European history often dated from 476 to 1453 A.D.

monotone A way of talking without raising or lowering the sound of your voice

oath A formal promise to do something

occultism A kind of supernatural power or magic

paranormal Something that cannot be explained by science

prop An object used by a performer to create a certain effect

ritual A set of actions performed according to social customs

second nature A skill or habit that is so familiar that it is automatic

special effect An illusion or visual trick used in movies and on television

stagecraft A collection of skills relating to performing

stage persona A role taken on by a performer

symbol Something that stands for something else

witchcraft The use of sorcery or magic

INDEX